The blissful journaling of:

Writing in a journal is such a great way to capture special thoughts and memories. It also helps spark my creativity. Hoping you find as much joy in keeping a journal as I do.

— hello angel

You just received some exciting news! Who's the first person you tell? Why?

_____

_____

_____

_____

_____

_____

_____

_____

_____

_____

_____

_____

_____

_____

_____

_____

_____

_____

_____

_____

What was your most successful New Year's resolution?

_____

_____

_____

_____

_____

_____

_____

_____

_____

_____

_____

_____

_____

_____

_____

_____

_____

_____

_____

_____

You run into your time-traveling future self. What do you ask yourself?

_____
_____
_____
_____
_____
_____
_____
_____
_____
_____
_____
_____
_____
_____
_____
_____
_____
_____
_____
_____

What have you worked the hardest for?

How do you cheer yourself up?

Oh darling, lets be adventurers

Love or money?

What have you stopped yourself from buying recently? Why?

_____

_____

_____

_____

_____

_____

_____

_____

_____

_____

_____

_____

_____

_____

_____

_____

_____

_____

_____

_____

_____

_____

_____

_____

_____

_____

_____

_____

_____

· ·

You have an unexpectedly free day. What do you do?

What was the best meal you've ever had?

For whom are you grateful?
When was the last time you talked to them?

_____

_____

_____

_____

_____

_____

_____

_____

_____

_____

_____

_____

_____

_____

_____

_____

_____

_____

_____

_____

Take a look around at your surroundings.
What are three things you can see right
now that you like?

_____
_____
_____
_____
_____
_____
_____
_____
_____
_____
_____
_____
_____
_____
_____
_____
_____
_____
_____
_____
_____
_____

What is your go-to activity when you want to procrastinate?

_____

_____

_____

_____

_____

_____

_____

_____

_____

_____

_____

_____

_____

_____

_____

_____

_____

_____

_____

_____

Dogs or cats?

_____
_____
_____
_____
_____
_____
_____
_____
_____
_____
_____
_____
_____
_____
_____
_____
_____
_____

What was the last compliment you gave someone? How was it received?

_____

_____

_____

_____

_____

_____

_____

_____

_____

_____

_____

_____

_____

_____

_____

_____

_____

_____

What color is your mood today?

When was the last time you cried? Why?

Never Give Up

What did you want to be when you grew up?
Did you change your mind along the way?

_____
_____
_____
_____
_____
_____
_____
_____
_____
_____
_____
_____
_____
_____
_____
_____
_____
_____
_____

How would your best friend describe you? Your mother? Your pet?

_____

_____

_____

_____

_____

_____

_____

_____

_____

_____

_____

_____

_____

_____

_____

_____

_____

_____

_____

You find a magic lamp, and the genie inside offers to change one thing in your life. What do you choose?

_____
_____
_____
_____
_____
_____
_____
_____
_____
_____
_____
_____
_____
_____
_____
_____
_____
_____
_____
_____
_____
_____
_____
_____

What kind of friend are you?

What is the best scent on Earth?

What is a class you would like to take?

What can you do better than anyone else?

You just got a promotion!
How would you like to celebrate?

What animal is most similar to you?

You can send your teenage self a letter with one piece of advice in it. What do you write?

What's the best thing to do when you're at home during a thunderstorm?

Set a goal for next month.
Set a goal for tomorrow.

What makes you unique?

What is your earliest memory?

If you could have dinner with any three people, alive or dead, who would you choose?

_____

_____

_____

_____

_____

_____

_____

_____

_____

_____

_____

_____

_____

_____

_____

_____

Who is your biggest hero? Why?

About the Artist

Angelea Van Dam of Hello Angel has drawn her entire life. This New Zealand artist is a graphic designer by trade, working out of her home as a freelancer. Her color style is every color under the sun and then she likes to pile on some more! Angelea wants to be in her studio making art almost all the time. It's what makes her happy. The fact that her art inspires others makes her doubly happy and motivates her to create so much more.

Color Your World with Hello Angel Coloring

ISBN 978-1-64178-004-9

Fox Chapel Publishing makes every effort to use environmentally friendly paper for printing.

© 2018 by Hello Angel/Artlicensing.com and Quiet Fox Designs, www.QuietFoxDesigns.com, an imprint of Fox Chapel Publishing, 800-457-9112, 903 Square Street, Mount Joy, PA 17552.

We are always looking for talented authors. To submit an idea, please send a brief inquiry to acquisitions@foxchapelpublishing.com.

Printed in China
First printing